Festivals *of the* World

CANADA

Gareth Stevens Publishing
MILWAUKEE

This book is dedicated to Brianne Jordana Wood

Written by
BOB BARLAS and **NORM TOMPSETT**

Edited by
SUSAN MCKAY

Designed by
LOO CHUAN MING

First published in North America in 1997 by
Gareth Stevens Publishing
1555 North RiverCenter Drive, Suite 201
Milwaukee, Wisconsin 53212 USA

For a free color catalog describing Gareth
Stevens' list of high-quality books and multimedia
programs, call
1-800-542-2595 (USA)
or 1-800-461-9120 (Canada).
Gareth Stevens Publishing's Fax: (414) 225-0377.
See our catalog, too, on the World Wide Web:
http://gsinc.com

© TIMES EDITIONS PTE LTD 1997
Originated and designed by
Times Books International
an imprint of Times Editions Pte Ltd
Times Centre, 1 New Industrial Road
Singapore 536196
Printed in Singapore

Library of Congress Cataloging-in-Publication Data:
Barlas, Robert.
Canada / by Robert Barlas and Norm Tompsett.
p. cm.—(Festivals of the world)
Includes bibliographical references (p. 27) and
index.
Summary: Describes how the culture of Canada is
reflected in its festivals.
ISBN 0-8368-1680-3 (1b)
1.Festivals—Canada—Juvenile literature. 2
Canada—Social life and customs—Juvenile
literature. [1. Festivals—Canada. 2. Canada—
Social life and customs.] I. Tompsett, Norm. II.
Title. III. Series.
GT4813.A2B37 1997
394.2'6971—dc20   96-29105

1 2 3 4 5 6 7 8 9 9 99 98 97

CONTENTS

It's Festival Time . . .

There are two official languages in Canada—French and English. In French you would call a festival a *fête* [fette]. But you'll also hear people speaking Greek, Italian, Mandarin, Punjabi, German, Japanese, and many other languages in Canada. And for each one of these languages there are all kinds of wild and wonderful festivals. So come along and join in the fun. It's fête time in Canada . . .

WHERE'S CANADA?

Canada is a huge country stretching from the northern border of the United States all the way to the Arctic Ocean, and from the island of Newfoundland all the way to Vancouver Island in the Pacific Ocean. Canada is divided into 10 provinces and two territories. The landscape of each province looks as different as the communities of people who live there. Ottawa is the capital of Canada.

Who are the Canadians?

The first people to live in Canada came almost 25,000 years ago during the **Ice Age**. After the ice melted, the people settled in small communities across North America. When the European explorers came looking for a route to India, they called these people Indians by mistake. Today, the original peoples are called the First Nations.

The maple leaf is the national symbol of Canada. The two red stripes on the flag represent the Pacific and Atlantic Oceans, two of the three oceans that Canada lies between.

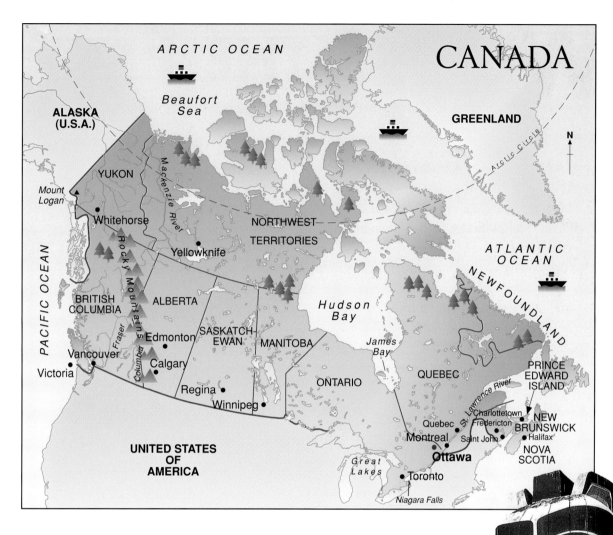

ARCTIC OCEAN

CANADA

Beaufort Sea

ALASKA (U.S.A.)

GREENLAND

YUKON

Mount Logan

Whitehorse

Mackenzie River

NORTHWEST TERRITORIES

Arctic Circle

N

Yellowknife

ATLANTIC OCEAN

PACIFIC OCEAN

Rocky Mountains

BRITISH COLUMBIA

ALBERTA

Fraser

Columbia

Edmonton

SASKATCH-EWAN

MANITOBA

Hudson Bay

James Bay

NEWFOUNDLAND

Vancouver

Calgary

Victoria

Regina

Winnipeg

ONTARIO

QUEBEC

St. Lawrence River

PRINCE EDWARD ISLAND

UNITED STATES OF AMERICA

Quebec

Montreal

Charlottetown

Fredericton

Saint John

NEW BRUNSWICK

Halifax

NOVA SCOTIA

Great Lakes

Ottawa

Toronto

Niagara Falls

After the Europeans claimed Canada, the face of the land began to change. Until the late 1800s, there were two main groups in Canada other than the First Nations—the British and the French. Most people lived in the eastern part of the country.

Later on, the government encouraged people from other countries to settle in the West by offering them free land. In the 1900s, many more people left their countries and made Canada their home. Today, Canada is a **multicultural** country proud of its many peoples.

For the First Nations of Canada, carving images in stone or wood is a way to record things, almost like writing down a story or memorizing it.

WHEN'S THE FÊTE?

WINTER

- **HANUKKAH** ✪ **CHRISTMAS**
- **KWANZAA**—The day when African Canadians sing, dance, and celebrate the harvest.
- **NEW YEAR'S DAY**
- **MIDWINTER FESTIVAL**—This festival begins five days after the new moon in January. The Iroquois Nation dress in traditional clothing and perform songs and dances important to their culture.
- **QUEBEC WINTER CARNIVAL**
- **CHINESE NEW YEAR**—People gather in the streets to watch lion and dragon dances and to set off fireworks.

SPRING

- **TULIP FESTIVAL** ✪ **MAPLE SYRUP FESTIVAL**
- **VICTORIA DAY**— Fireworks are set off in the sky all across Canada to celebrate Queen Victoria's birthday.
- **ST. JEAN BAPTISTE DAY**—Thousands of people crowd the streets of Quebec in giant parades to honor John the Baptist. This is also a day for French Canadians to celebrate their culture.

Want to really rock 'n roll? Come to the Calgary Stampede on page 20.

SUMMER

- ✪ **CANADA DAY** ✪ **LOUIS RIEL DAY**—This is a day when the First Nations and French Canadians celebrate the uprising of Louis Riel against the Canadian government to protest the settling of their lands.
- ✪ **KLONDIKE DAYS**—People take part in log-sawing and rock-lifting contests to see who is the King of the Klondike. The Klondike is a river in Alberta where gold was discovered in 1896.
- ✪ **CALGARY STAMPEDE**
- ✪ **NATIONAL UKRAINIAN FESTIVAL**—In addition to watching the lively Ukrainian dances, visitors to this festival get to eat *kolach* [KO-latch]—Ukrainian bread with salt on top—to celebrate the spice of life.
- ✪ **CARIBANA**—A week-long Caribbean festival. Traveling bands take to the streets, and more than 6,000 Canadians from the Caribbean islands participate.

AUTUMN

- ✪ **WILD RICE HARVEST**—First Nations children in Manitoba, Saskatchewan, and Ontario get to take time off school to help gather the wild rice. After it has all been gathered, there is a huge feast to celebrate the harvest.
- ✪ **THANKSGIVING** ✪ **OKTOBERFEST** ✪ **HALLOWEEN**
- ✪ **REMEMBRANCE DAY**—People wear red poppies to remember the soldiers who died in World War I. Poppies grow in the cemeteries in Europe where Canadian soldiers are buried.

THE QUEBEC WINTER CARNIVAL

It's very, very cold in Quebec City in February, and there's lots of snow and ice. That means only one thing to the people who live there—it's time to have a party!

Quebec City has been having a winter party—called the *Carnaval du Québec* [car-na-val dew kay-BECK] in French—since 1954. Carnival's symbol is a pudgy snowman that wears a red hat and sash. The snowman is called *Bonhomme Carnaval* [bun-UM car-na-val], which means Gentleman Carnival, and it comes to life during Carnival. In fact, it appears at most of the festival's events.

It's show time!

On Friday night when Carnival begins, there is a special show for all the spectators. The show features singing, dancing, and performances of folk stories of the French people in Quebec. More than half of the people in Quebec speak French. French Canadians have a unique culture and history.

Bonhomme Carnaval is ready to party! Lots of other cities in Canada have winter carnivals, too, but the Quebec Winter Carnival is the biggest winter festival in the world. More than one million people come to join in each year!

The Festival Queen

The main event of the Carnival is the crowning of the Festival Queen by Bonhomme Carnaval at a special ceremony. A new queen is chosen every year from among many local girls who try out for this special honor. A formal ball is held at the castle in Quebec to celebrate the crowning of the queen.

The crowning of the Carnival Queen is one of the main events at Carnival. Another event is the *Soirée de la Bougie* [swa-ray de la boo-jee], which means Night of the Candle. On this night the whole city is lit up by thousands of candles.

Snow baths and canoe races

Two of the funniest events of the Quebec Winter Carnival are the snow bath and the canoe race. In spite of the fact that it is very cold and there is lots of snow on the ground, many of the people at the Carnival take part in the snow bath. Dressed only in their bathing suits, they roll around in the snow until they are so cold they have to stop! Over 100 people take part in this very popular event every year. The canoe race goes across the St. Lawrence River, which is almost completely frozen at that time of year.

Canoe racers at Carnival have to fight the strong current and the ice to get across to the other side of the St. Lawrence River.

The skyline of the city of Quebec is dominated by a real castle, Château Frontenac [sha-TOH fron-tuh-KNACK]. It sits on top of a hill so you can see it from almost any point in the city.

Join in the fun

Besides canoe racing and bathing in the snow, there is also a winter softball tournament, ice wall climbing, and a torchlit ski parade. During Carnival, the entire city of Quebec is decorated with streamers and lights.

The centerpiece is a huge ice castle made out of more than 2,500 blocks of ice. This takes more than a month to make. Surrounding it are hundreds of ice sculptures, made by the people taking part in Carnival. There are also huge fireworks displays, which are very popular.

Sculptors from all over the world come to compete in the annual Ice Sculpting Competition. Contestants sculpt everything from animals to airplanes.

Eat, drink, and be merry!

Of course, there are lots of good things to eat and drink, too, like *tourtière* [TOR-tee-air], which is a kind of meat pie, *poutine* [poo-TEEN], french fries with a special gravy, and *Caribou* [carry-boo], a drink made with red wine which people carry around with them in special hollow canes so that they can have a sip whenever they want! Tourtière and poutine are famous French Canadian foods. Caribou is supposed to be one of the best ways to keep out the cold of winter during Carnival.

Think about this
The French are known to have a great *joie de vivre* [jooa duh veevre], or joy of living, that comes alive during Carnival. Are there any famous carnivals near where you live? If so, what do people do at those carnivals? Is there any snow?

There is always lots of laughter and noise during Carnival. Along the streets of Quebec City you can buy your very own Carnival trumpet. When you blow into these red plastic trumpets, they make a very loud noise. Throughout the 10 days you can hear the sounds of the trumpets day and night.

MAPLE SYRUP FESTIVALS

Something that Canadians think of as very special to their country is maple syrup. They put it on their pancakes for breakfast, make ice cream with it, and even turn it into a special kind of butter or candy.

Maple syrup is made from the sap of the hard maple tree. The sap is taken from the tree each spring just as the winter is finishing and the days begin to get warmer. Collecting the sap is called "sugaring off" and is celebrated as a festival in small towns all over Canada in March or April.

If you pour hot syrup on the snow just after it has been boiled, it becomes sticky and chewy, almost like taffy. Then you can roll it onto a stick and eat it like a sucker.

How is maple syrup made?

As spring approaches, people who want to make maple syrup put a special tap, or **spigot,** into the trunk of their maple trees. A bucket is hung underneath the spigot to collect the sticky liquid that flows out of the tree. This liquid is called sap. Sometimes the taps are connected to a hose that runs from the **sugar bush**, where the trees are, to the sugar shack nearby. The sugar shack, which is often a flimsy building made of plywood with a tin roof, is where the maple syrup is made. When the sap arrives at the shack, it is put into a large tub and a fire is lit underneath it. The sap is boiled until all the water has evaporated. What is left over is put into bottles or tins, ready to be poured on your pancakes!

This is a traditional sugar shack. Today sap is usually collected mechanically, and the syrup is produced in a factory. It tastes just as good, but it certainly isn't as fun to visit a factory as it is to visit a sugar shack!

When the sap first comes out of the tree, it is sweet, but it is still very thin. It is so thin that it takes about 40 gallons (150 l) of sap to make only 1 gallon (4 l) of syrup.

Spring fever

The running of the sap in the maple trees happens at the same time every year, so people think of it as a sign that spring is coming and celebrate it with a festival. Many small towns and villages where a lot of sugar maple trees grow hold a special event at that time of year. In the small town of Warkworth in the province of Ontario, there are several activities that people can join in to celebrate the running of the maple sap and the beginning of spring. Keep reading and you'll find out what some of them are.

Sleigh rides

One of the most popular activities at maple syrup festivals is a special horse-drawn sleigh ride. The ride goes from the village into the sugar bush, where the maple trees and the sugar shack are. In the sugar bush, visitors can see the maple syrup being made and even buy some to take home.

As soon as the coldest part of winter is over, Canadian families head for the outdoors. Maple syrup festivals are just one of the many ways to have fun. At the beginning of spring there is also an Apple Blossom Festival and a Tulip Festival.

In the olden days, before roads were built and cars were invented, the only way to get around in the snow was by horse-drawn sleigh or on snowshoes. These days, sleigh rides are just for fun. If you really want to get around in the country during winter, you've got to use a **skidoo**, or snowmobile. These are a lot like motorcycles, with skis instead of wheels.

On your mark, get set, go!

Special contests are also held. In the log-sawing contest, the object is to see who is the quickest at sawing a big log in half using an old-fashioned saw. These two-handled saws are often so heavy that it takes two strong men to lift one! Taking part in a snowshoe race means putting on special shoes, which look like tennis rackets, and then seeing who can run the fastest over a stretch of snow.

Everyone enjoys taking part in the special events at a maple syrup festival. Children are especially fond of eating the sweet, sticky maple candy and syrup. It sounds like going to a festival like this one would be great fun for the whole family, doesn't it?

In the log-sawing contest, contestants are timed using a stopwatch. The team that saws through the log fastest wins a prize.

Square dancing is one of the things people do at a maple syrup festival. Dancers have to follow the instructions given to them by a **caller**. The caller has a series of commands that he uses to tell the dancers what to do next. It takes a lot of practice to listen to the music and follow the commands at the same time!

Think about this

A maple syrup festival is just one way to celebrate spring. Is there anything special that you do to welcome back the spring?

CELEBRATING CANADA

July 1st is Canada's birthday. On this day in 1867, four different provinces on the eastern side of the continent—Nova Scotia, New Brunswick, Quebec, and Ontario—agreed to join together to form one country that they called Canada. This new country had its capital at the city of Bytown, which was soon renamed Ottawa. Since 1867, Canada has added six more provinces—Prince Edward Island, Manitoba, Saskatchewan, Alberta, British Columbia, and Newfoundland. Today, Canada has a total of 10 provinces.

July 1st is a very special day of the year when Canadians of all different backgrounds celebrate their pride in being Canadian. Every year the Royal Canadian Mounted Police (the Mounties), Canada's national police force, put on a special show, and fireworks are set off over the Parliament Buildings in Ottawa.

Happy birthday to you

Every July 1st, Canadians all over the country celebrate Canada's birthday in lots of different ways. The biggest party is in Ottawa, where the Prime Minister makes a speech. There is also a special ceremony where newcomers to the country receive their Canadian citizenship. Afterward, the entertainment begins with the Mounties putting on their famous Musical Ride, a routine on horseback set to music (turn back to page 16 to see the Musical Ride). Canadian rock musicians put on special outdoor concerts, and the whole day finishes with a huge fireworks display. Many of the people who go to Ottawa to celebrate wear special paper hats with red and white maple leaves on them, the symbol of Canada.

This boy is having his face painted with a favorite summer fruit—watermelon. If you were in Canada on Canada Day, how would you have your face painted?

A day for all Canadians

Ottawa is not the only place where Canadians celebrate their country's birthday. Toronto, Canada's largest city, has a parade through the center of the city and a free picnic for anyone who wants to come. People of all different **ethnic** groups put on their national dress for the glittering parade. Afterward, everyone gathers at the city's Exhibition Place to watch the shows and eat free food until late into the night. Other big Canadian cities like Halifax, Montreal, Winnipeg, Edmonton, and Vancouver (find these on the map on page 5) also have special parties for their citizens on Canada Day.

Immigrants to Canada, such as these Japanese-Canadians, are encouraged to hold on to their culture and traditions even after they have become Canadian citizens. This government policy is known as "multiculturalism."

Celebration time

Everybody celebrates Canada's birthday in their own way. All over the country, in big towns and small villages, people get together to show that they are happy to be Canadian. People gather in local parks or town squares where adults listen to speeches made by well-known local people and watch musical entertainment.

There are also lots of activities for children, such as face painting, sack races, and soap box derbies. Some of the other attractions include watching clowns and magicians perform tricks, stunts, and magic. Since Canadians come from all over the world, one of the special features is the ethnic food stalls. Here you can enjoy foods from lots of different countries. And because Canada Day falls in the middle of summer, there are usually lots of strawberries and watermelon for everyone to eat!

The whole family enjoys Canada Day and celebrates everything that makes being Canadian really special. How would you like to come to Canada next year on July 1st and join in the fun?

Think about this

What day of the year do Americans celebrate their pride in their country? What are the similarities between this day and Canada Day? What are the differences?

What a bunch of rowdy characters! These musicians are just a few of the many live entertainers who perform on Canada Day. If you're lucky, you can see some of the more famous Canadian rock stars who give outdoor concerts. Anyone can go, and sometimes you don't even need to buy tickets.

THE CALGARY STAMPEDE

Do you know what a **rodeo** is? Every year during the month of July, the city of Calgary in western Canada hosts the biggest one in the world! Cowboys from all over the globe come to Calgary to show off their skills in taming wild horses and fierce bulls, wrestling with young steers, throwing the lasso, and racing horse-drawn chuckwagons. This is known as the Calgary Stampede.

The Calgary Stampede started out as a sideshow to attract people to the annual agricultural fairs, where farmers displayed fresh produce, such as grapes.

In the summer and fall, cities and towns all over Canada hold big agricultural fairs. These are to celebrate farmers and ranchers, who display the food they've grown and the special skills they have. The Calgary Stampede is part of one of these fairs, but the Wild West rodeo events that take place in Calgary make it a very special festival, and a very exciting one, too!

During the Calgary Stampede, visitors and Calgarians dress as cowboys from the tops of their hats to the tips of their boots. Cowboy boots are not only part of the outfit, they keep your feet clean in case you step in something you shouldn't. And with all those cows and horses around, it's pretty hard not to!

Yihah!

The cowboys show off their skills in three riding contests called "roughstock" events. In the contests, the cowboys have to stay on the animals they are riding for as long as they can. The three riding events are saddle bronc riding, bareback riding, and bull riding.

Saddle broncs are wild, untamed horses that jump and twist around, trying to throw their riders off their backs. The cowboy sits in a special saddle and has to stay on for as long as he can with only one rein to control the horse.

In bareback riding, the cowboys have no saddle at all. All they can use is a special harness like a suitcase handle to keep them from falling off!

The most exciting of the riding events is bull riding, where the cowboys have to try and stay on the back of untamed bulls. The bulls weigh about 15 times more than their riders!

Since the riders are only allowed to hold on with one hand in saddle bronc riding, they use the other one to try to balance themselves. But hanging on is no easy task, and many riders stay on for less than eight seconds. The horses are picked for their stubbornness to training and their habit of throwing riders.

21

In the nick of time

There are also three timed events—calf roping, steer wrestling, and barrel racing. In these events, the cowboys have to do a special task in the fastest possible time. In the calf roping contest, the cowboys use a lasso to catch a calf that is running as fast as it can away from them. Once they've caught it, they tie three of its legs together so it can't run away.

Steers are young cows. In steer wrestling the cowboy has to catch a cow by its horns, turn it over onto its back, and hold it until it can't move anymore.

Barrel racing is the only event for cowgirls at the Calgary Stampede. The riders have to race their horses around three barrels on a special track. The fastest one is the winner.

Chuckwagon racing

Besides these rodeo events, there are also the chuckwagon races. They are great fun to watch. **Chuckwagon** is the name for the big wooden carts that cowboys used to live in when they were camping out on the open range. Now the old chuckwagons used on the farms have been replaced by modern machines, but every year there is still a special race for them at the Calgary Stampede. It is very exciting to see them going as fast as they can around the race track, sometimes almost tipping over as they turn the corners!

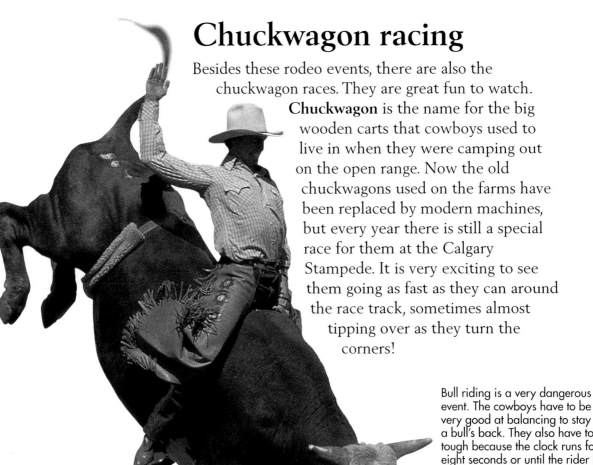

Bull riding is a very dangerous event. The cowboys have to be very good at balancing to stay on a bull's back. They also have to be tough because the clock runs for eight seconds or until the rider has been thrown from the bull. Ouch!

And that's not all . . .

The whole Calgary Stampede lasts for 10 days during July. In addition to the rodeo events, there are other events all over the city of Calgary at the same time. They include pancake breakfasts, square dancing in the streets, colorful parades, and special country music concerts in the parks. The Calgary Stampede is certainly one of the most exciting festivals in Canada, isn't it?

Chuckwagon racing has been going on since the time of the original settlers of the Wild West. The cowboys used to race their chuckwagons to see which was the fastest. The team of four horses pulling the wagon had to work very hard!

You can enjoy all kinds of Western foods at the Stampede. The biggest meal for a cowboy is usually breakfast, with ham, bacon, hash browns, eggs, pancakes, and toast.

Think about this

The original cowboys came from Mexico. Pioneers from Canada and the United States visited Mexico and learned about cattle farming. What we think of as cowboy hats today were originally *sombreros* [som-BRAY-ros]—wide-brimmed, floppy Mexican hats.

23

POWWOW

After the settlers from Europe came to North America, many things changed for the people of the First Nations. In some cases the settlers took their lands away from them, and many of their ceremonies and festivals were banned as well.

Today many of the First Nation festivals are being celebrated again in the way they were many years ago. Different Nations celebrate in different ways, but they all have some form of festival called a **powwow**. People dress in traditional clothing and eat traditional food. Everyone is welcome at a powwow.

The Grand Entry

Before any powwow begins, there is a ceremony called the Grand Entry. A parade of people comes toward the special circle where the dancing and drumming take place. The leaders of this parade carry the Eagle Staff, the oldest of the First Nation symbols. They are followed by the flag bearers, who carry the flags of all the Nations who are taking part in the powwow. Drummers beat a special **tattoo** as the flags are raised, and the whole group sings to celebrate the powwow. The final part of the Grand Entry is the offering of a special prayer.

In a powwow feast, food is cooked by women and served by the men of the community. Some food is sprinkled with tobacco and put on the ground to honor Mother Earth and her gift of food. Then everyone eats, the oldest starting first, followed by the children, the women, and finally the men.

Dancing

Many of the dances performed at powwows are thousands of years old. They are part of the ancient traditions of the First Nations. Some of the dances celebrate special events. The Victory Dance was performed to celebrate a successful hunt. Dances can also tell a story from history, like the Snake Dance, and some are just for show. In the Fancy Dance, the dancers combine fast twisting and spinning with modern dance steps. There are also social dances, such as the Grass Dance, which is danced in teams of men and women. Even the children sometimes take part.

Drumming, dancing, and singing are very important parts of a powwow. The First Nations believe that the drum is the heartbeat of their people and of Mother Earth. Drums are sacred to the people who play them. They are treated with the same kind of respect given a very important person.

THINGS FOR YOU TO DO

A re there any winter carnivals near where you live? If not, why don't you organize your own winter carnival? Here are some great ideas to get you started on your very own festival of snow!

Make a snow sculpture

We're not talking about a simple snowman here. You may need a shovel for this one. Gather as much snow together as you can, and start to build something. You should have a pretty good idea of what you want to make before you get started. You'll probably need some tools to help you carve whatever sculpture you have planned.

Make an igloo

Make it big enough for more than one person so you can invite your friends and family to join you inside your new home. Start by making a pile of snowballs. Or use a square box and fill it with snow to form cubes. Be sure to leave a hole on one side so you can get in and out easily. And maybe one on the roof, too, so the light can get through. Once you've finished building your igloo, ask an adult to light a candle so you can heat it up. If you were a real Canadian Inuit, you might have a meal of whale blubber or **bannock**, pancakes made from rice and flour. But if you can't get your hands on these, try a few snacks from home.

Make a snow snake

If you live near a steep hill or a slope, you and your friends can play Snow Snakes. This is a traditional Iroquois game. To play it you'll need to make your own snow snake. Look for a smooth tree branch about 4 feet (1.2 m) long. You can use an old broom handle if you can't find a good branch. Strip off the bark from the branch and smooth out any rough spots with sandpaper. Now paint a few designs on the head of the snake with paints. Once you've finished making your snake, you're ready to play Snow Snakes. Make a track on a steep slope by dragging your boot through the snow and then packing the snow down hard. Now, one by one, send your snakes down the hill. The snake that travels the farthest is the winner.

Things to look for in your library

Canada Celebrates Multiculturalism. Bobbie Kalman (Crabtree, 1993).
Canada Je t'aime/I Love You. Roch Carrier (Tundra Books, 1991).
Discovering American Indian Music (video).
Native Peoples. Smith (Stoddart Publications, 1994).
Postcards from Canada. Zoe Dawson (Raintree/Steck Vaughn, 1995).
Pow Wow (video).
Songs of the Inuit (compact disk).
White Fang. Jack London (Watermill Press, 1992).

MAKE A DREAMCATCHER

A dreamcatcher is a brightly colored, traditional decoration made by the people of the First Nations. It is usually hung in a sleeping area. The dreamcatcher is supposed to catch all the bad dreams while the feathers let the good dreams come through to the person sleeping.

You will need:
1. An embroidery hoop
2. A ball of brightly colored yarn
3. Wooden beads
4. Feathers
5. Scissors
6. Paints
7. Paintbrush

1 Paint the embroidery hoop with the paints. Let it dry for about 15 minutes.

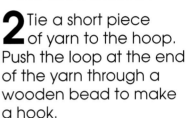

2 Tie a short piece of yarn to the hoop. Push the loop at the end of the yarn through a wooden bead to make a hook.

3 Thread a few beads onto your yarn. Tie the end to the top of the hoop and gradually unwind the ball of yarn with the beads attached by taking it to a point opposite the hook. Loop the yarn once or twice around the hoop and then stretch it across the circle again to a different point. Repeat this step several times until you've made a pattern. Each time your yarn crosses another bit of yarn, wind it around. This makes an uneven pattern. Push a bead up to the top of the yarn when you're ready to place it in your pattern. When you've made a nice pattern, cut the yarn and tie it to the hoop to make sure that it all stays in place.

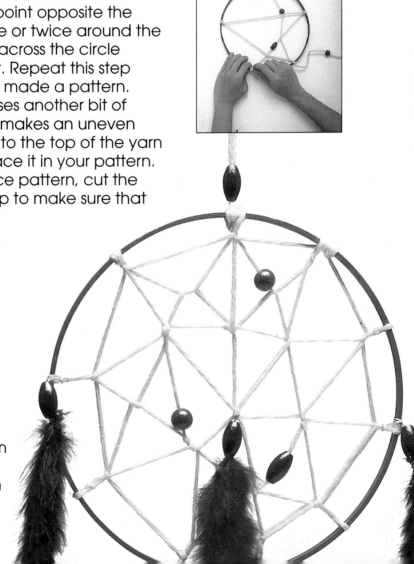

4 Attach a piece of yarn and a bead to the feathers and tie them to the dreamcatcher wherever you want them to be.

Make Pancakes with Maple Syrup

Pancakes are very popular for breakfast in Canada, especially during festivals. They are often eaten with eggs, bacon or sausages—and, of course, lots of maple syrup!

You will need:

1. 2 eggs
2. 2 cups (480 ml) buttermilk (or sour milk)
3. 1 teaspoon baking soda
4. 2 cups (280 g) sifted flour
5. 2 teaspoons baking powder
6. ½ teaspoon of salt
7. 6 tablespoons butter or margarine
8. A bottle or tin of real maple syrup
9. 2 mixing bowls
10. A wooden spoon
11. Measuring cups
12. Measuring spoons
13. A whisk
14. A spatula
15. A frying pan

2 Put the other ingredients (except the butter and syrup) into another bowl and mix them together.

1 Break the eggs into a large bowl and beat them well. Add the buttermilk and mix it all together.

4 Have an adult help you melt two tablespoons of the butter in a large frying pan or a griddle over medium heat. Pour the batter into the frying pan, making it into circles. Cook the pancakes until bubbles start to show all over the surface. Take a spatula and turn the pancakes over. Cook for two more minutes. Continue until you have used up all of the batter.

3 Add the dry ingredients to the egg and buttermilk mixture and beat it until it is smooth.

5 Put two or three pancakes on each plate and pour the maple syrup over the top. Pancakes are great for breakfast, but you can eat them at any time of day!

GLOSSARY

bannock, 27 — Pancakes made from rice and flour, eaten by the Inuit.
caller, 15 — The person who calls out the instructions in a square dance.
chuckwagon, 22 — Wooden carts that cowboys lived and cooked in when they were out on the open range.
ethnic, 18 — Connected to different racial or cultural groups.
Ice Age, 4 — A time when most of the northern hemisphere was under ice.
multicultural, 5 — Having many different cultures.
powwow, 24 — A gathering of Nations to celebrate their history and culture.
rodeo, 20 — A place where cowboys gather to show off their skills.
skidoo, 14 — A sleigh with a motor and skis that moves over the snow.
spigot, 13 — A tap to control the flow of sap from the maple trees.
sugar bush, 13 — A grove of sugar-maples.
tattoo, 24 — The beat of a drum.

INDEX